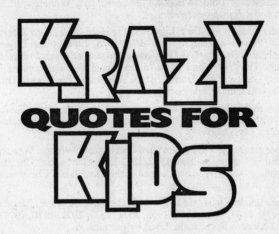

KRAZY QUOTES FOR KIDS

VERN McLELLAN

Illustrated by
Nate Owens

HARVEST HOUSE PUBLISHERS
Eugene, Oregon 97402

KRAZY QUOTES FOR KIDS

Copyright © 1993 by Vernon McLellan
Published by Harvest House Publishers
Eugene, Oregon 97402

Library of Congress Cataloging-in-Publication Data

McLellan, Vernon K.
    Krazy quotes for kids / Vern McLellan.
      p.   cm.
    Summary: A collection of one-line jokes with serious intent, thematically linked with proverbs in the Bible. Example: "Kids who fiddle around seldom get to lead the orchestra. (Prov 14:23)"
    ISBN 1-56507-070-4
    1. Wit and humor, Juvenile. 2. Proverbs—Juvenile literature. 3. Quotations. [1. Proverbs. 2. Conduct of life—Wit and humor. 3. Christian life—Wit and humor. 4. Wit and humor.] I. Title.
PN6163.M29   1993   92-43663
818'.5402—dc20   CIP
                                           AC

Printed in the United States of America.

To my grand kids:

Jon, Julie, Jaclyn,
Emmalee, and Evan

Introduction

Exactly what is a quote (or proverb)? (Or, as I call them in this book, a krazy quote?) Here are some good definitions:

> A simple teaching on an everyday problem.

> A small statement teaching enormous truth.

> A flash of light into a dark, unknown place.

How useful are these krazy quotes? For more than 20 years, I have seen kids everywhere laugh at and enjoy quotes like the ones in this book. And I'm sure you, too, will find these short sayings of wisdom great for sharing with your family and friends.

Many of the quotes in this book have come from Asia, Europe, the Middle East, and Australia. Others appeared anonymously in newspapers, magazines, church bulletins, or on billboards, restaurant place-mats, and truck doors.

With every quote is an important word of wisdom from the Bible—wisdom that comes from the Psalms and Proverbs. I believe you will find in this book many insights that will help you to become a wise person in all that you do in your home, school, and church.

—Vern McLellan

Kids who bring sunshine into the lives of others cannot keep it from themselves.

Proverbs 17:22

A cheerful heart does good like medicine, but a broken spirit makes one sick.

Kids who roll up their sleeves seldom lose their shirts.

Proverbs 15:19

A lazy fellow has trouble all through life; the good man's path is easy!

Kids who don't stand for something will fall for anything.

Proverbs 4:7

Determination to be wise is the first step to becoming wise! And with your wisdom, develop common sense and good judgment.

Kids who aim at nothing are sure to hit it.

Proverbs 17:24

Wisdom is the main pursuit of sensible men, but a fool's goals are at the ends of the earth!

Kids who think by the inch and talk by the yard deserve to be kicked by the foot.

Proverbs 10:19

Don't talk so much. You keep putting your foot in your mouth. Be sensible and turn off the flow!

Kids who have a good opinion of themselves are likely poor judges of human nature.

Proverbs 26:12

There is one thing worse than a fool, and that is a man who is conceited.

Kids who fiddle around seldom get to lead the orchestra.

Proverbs 14:23

Work brings profit; talk brings poverty!

Kids who gossip usually wind up in their own mouth traps.

Proverbs 26:20,22

Fire goes out for lack of fuel, and tensions disappear when gossip stops.

14

Kids who want to eat the kernel must first crack the nut.

Proverbs 13:4

Lazy people want much but get little,
while the diligent are prospering.

15

Kids who ask a question may look like fools for five minutes, but kids who never ask a question remain fools forever.

Proverbs 15:14

A wise man is hungry for truth, while the mocker feeds on trash.

Kids who faithfully pray for rain should carry an umbrella.

Proverbs 15:29

The Lord is far from the wicked, but he hears the prayers of the righteous.

Kids who drive too fast into the next county may wind up in the next world.

Proverbs 16:25

Before every man there lies a wide and pleasant road he thinks is right, but it ends in death.

Kids who pull on the oars don't have time to rock the boat.

Proverbs 22:29

Do you know a hard-working man? He shall be successful and stand before kings!

Kids who keep a cool head stay out of hot water.

Proverbs 16:32

It is better to be slow-tempered than famous; it is better to have self-control than to control an army.

Kids who have time to lean have time to clean.

Proverbs 16:27

Idle hands are the devil's workshop; idle lips are his mouthpiece.

Kids who walk on clouds leave too many things up in the air.

Proverbs 27:12

A sensible man watches for problems ahead and prepares to meet them. The simpleton never looks, and suffers the consequences.

Kids who want to steal second base must get their foot off first.

Ecclesiastes 5:5

It is far better not to say you'll do something than to say you will and then not do it.

Kids who want good luck fishing must get there yesterday when the fish were biting.

Ecclesiastes 3:1

There is a right time for everything.

Kids who lead a checkered life often end up in a striped suit.

Proverbs 1:17

When a bird sees a trap being set, it stays away.

Kids who want an idea of their worth should count their friends.

Proverbs 18:19

It is harder to win back the friendship of an offended brother than to capture a fortified city. His anger shuts you out like iron bars.

Kids who snooze looze (lose).

Proverbs 10:5

A wise youth makes hay while the sun shines, but what a shame to see a lad who sleeps away his hour of opportunity.

Kids who show off usually get showed up at the showdown.

Proverbs 22:4

True humility and respect for the Lord lead a man to riches, honor and long life.

Kids who raise the roof usually don't have much in the attic.

Proverbs 12:23

A wise man doesn't display his knowledge, but a fool displays his foolishness.

Kids who want to climb the ladder of success must take their hands out of their pockets.

Proverbs 13:4

Lazy people want much but get little, while the diligent are prospering.

Kids who are wrapped up in themselves are very small packages.

Proverbs 29:23

Pride ends in a fall, while humility brings honor.

Kids who have a sore throat should be thankful they are not a giraffe.

Psalm 92:1

It is good to say, "Thank you" to the Lord, to sing praises to the God who is above all gods.

Kids who live by killing time die with it.

Psalm 146:3,4

Don't look to men for help; their greatest leaders fail; for every man must die. His breathing stops, life ends, and in a moment all he planned for himself is ended.

Kids who say nothing is impossible should try to dribble a football.

Proverbs 21:5

Steady plodding brings prosperity;
hasty speculation brings poverty.

Kids who want to save face should stop shooting it off.

Proverbs 17:27,28

The man of few words and settled mind is wise; therefore, even a fool is thought to be wise when he is silent. It pays him to keep his mouth shut.

Kids who become a judge between two friends lose one.

Proverbs 27:6,9

Wounds from a friend are better than kisses from an enemy!....Friendly suggestions are as pleasant as perfume.

Kids who first do not succeed should read the instructions.

Proverbs 8:10,11

My instruction is more valuable than silver or gold. For the value of wisdom is far above rubies; nothing can be compared with it.

Kids who live it up often have trouble living it down.

Proverbs 15:16

Better a little with reverence for God, than great treasure and trouble with it.

Kids who want to soar like eagles must avoid running with turkeys.

Proverbs 24:3,4

Any enterprise is built by wise planning, becomes strong through common sense, and profits wonderfully by keeping abreast of the facts.

Kids who want a long friendship should develop a short memory.

1 Corinthians 13:5

[Love] does not hold grudges and will hardly even notice when others do wrong.

Kids who are lazy can't get the bed off their back.

Proverbs 20:13

If you love sleep, you will end in poverty. Stay awake, work hard, and there will be plenty to eat!

Kids who jump to conclusions cannot always expect happy landings.

Proverbs 18:13

What a shame–yes, how stupid!–to decide before knowing the facts!

Kids who oversleep cannot make their dreams come true.

Ecclesiastes 5:7

Dreaming instead of doing is foolishness, and there is ruin in a flood of empty words; fear God instead.

Kids who growl all day live a dog's life.

Proverbs 15:4

Gentle words cause life and health;
griping brings discouragement.

Kids who plan to drink and drive should kiss mother goodbye.

Proverbs 21:16

The man who strays away from common sense will end up dead!

45

Kids who lack courage think with their legs.

Proverbs 18:14

A man's courage can sustain his broken body, but when courage dies, what hope is left?

Kids who seek a friend without fault remain without one.

Matthew 7:3

Why worry about a speck in the eye of a brother when you have a board in your own?

Kids who can enjoy the scenery even when they have to take a detour are truly content.

Proverbs 4:18

The good man walks along in the ever-brightening light of God's favor; the dawn gives way to morning splendor.

Kids who have their ducks in a row will not quack up.

Psalm 37:23

The steps of good men are directed by the Lord. He delights in each step they take.

49

Kids who bury their talents are making a grave mistake.

Proverbs 28:13

A man who refuses to admit his mistakes can never be successful. But if he confesses and forsakes them, he gets another chance.

Kids who say they can, can!

Proverbs 4:7

Determination to be wise is the first step toward becoming wise! And with your wisdom, develop common sense and good judgment.

Kids who want to hear money jingle in their pockets must "shake a leg."

Proverbs 14:23 (NIV)

All hard work brings a profit, but mere talk leads only to poverty.

Kids who want to get their name in the newspaper should cross the street reading one.

Proverbs 14:16

A wise man is cautious and avoids danger;
a fool plunges ahead with great confidence.

Kids who do not know where they are going will soon discover that any road will take them there.

Proverbs 14:15

A prudent man checks to see where he is going.

Kids who think time heals all things should try sitting in a doctor's office.

Proverbs 25:15

Through patience a ruler can be persuaded, and a gentle tongue can break a bone.

Kids who expect something for nothing will have to wait until Easter falls on a Tuesday.

Proverbs 12:9

It is better to get your hands dirty–and eat, than to be too proud to work–and starve.

Kids who keep their mouth shut stop a lot of people from jumping down their throat.

Proverbs 15:28

A good man thinks before he speaks;
the evil man pours out his evil words
without a thought.

Kids who find them-selves in a hole can always look up at the stars.

Philippians 4:12

I have learned the secret of content-ment in every situation, whether it be a full stomach or hunger, plenty or want.

Kids who want to leave footprints in the sands of time should wear work boots.

Proverbs 12:24

Work hard and become a leader; be lazy and never succeed.

Kids who want to get into WHO'S WHO must first learn WHAT'S WHAT.

Proverbs 1:8,9

Only fools refuse to be taught. Listen to your father and mother. What you learn from them will stand you in good stead; it will gain you many honors.

Kids who are wise by day are not fools by night.

ALWAYS THERE BATTERIES

Proverbs 9:11,12

I, Wisdom, will make the hours of your day more profitable and the years of your life more fruitful. Wisdom is its own reward, and if you scorn her, you hurt only yourself.

Kids who feed their faith will starve their doubts to death.

Proverbs 3:4,5

If you want favor with both God and man, and a reputation for good judgment and common sense, then trust the Lord completely; don't ever trust yourself.

Kids who invite trouble always complain when it accepts.

Proverbs 19:3

A man may ruin his chances by his own foolishness and then blame it on the Lord!

Kids who think they are in the groove are actually in the rut.

Proverbs 16:17

The path of the godly leads away from evil; he who follows that path is safe.

Kids who fall in love with themselves will have no competition.

Proverbs 15:33

Humility and reverence for the Lord
will make you both wise and honored.

Kids who have to eat their own words never ask for a second helping.

Proverbs 21:23

Keep your mouth closed and you'll stay out of trouble.

Kids who want to fool the fox must rise early.

Song of Solomon 2:15

The little foxes are ruining the vine-yards. Catch them, for the grapes are all in blossom.

Kids who hesitate never become leaders.

Ecclesiastes 11:4

If you wait for perfect conditions, you will never get anything done.

Kids who help dig others out of their troubles find a place to bury their own.

Proverbs 21:21

The man who tries to be good, loving and kind finds life, righteousness and honor.

Kids who want to leap high walls must make a long run.

Psalm 18:29

Now in [God's] strength I can scale any wall, attack any troop.

Kids who do not pray when the sun shines will not know how to pray when the storm hits.

Isaiah 55:6

Seek the Lord while you can find him.
Call upon him now while he is near.

Kids who throw dirt lose ground.

Proverbs 10:14

A wise man holds his tongue. Only a fool blurts out everything he knows; that only leads to sorrow and trouble.

Kids who itch for success must be willing to scratch for it.

Psalm 37:5

Commit everything you do to the Lord.
Trust him to help you do it and he will.

73

Kids who want to make a splash in the puddle of life must be willing to jump.

Deuteronomy 31:6

Be strong! Be courageous! Do not be afraid.... For the Lord your God will be with you. He will neither fail you nor forsake you.

Kids who lie down with the dogs will get up with the fleas.

Proverbs 13:20

Be with wise men and become wise. Be with evil men and become evil.

Kids who overeat break the feed limit.

Proverbs 23:19,20

O my son, be wise and stay in God's paths; don't carouse with drunkards and gluttons, for they are on their way to poverty.

Kids who continually pat themselves on the back run the risk of dislocating their shoulder.

Proverbs 29:23

Pride ends in a fall, while humility brings honor.

Kids who cry over spilt milk should condense it.

Ecclesiastes 3:1,4

There is a right time for everything....a time to cry, a time to laugh.

Kids who get to the end of their ropes should tie a knot and hang on.

Joshua 1:9

Yes, be bold and strong! Banish fear and doubt! For remember, the Lord your God is with you wherever you go.

Kids who want eggs must be willing to endure cackling hens.

Psalm 30:5 (NKJV)

Weeping may endure for a night, but joy comes in the morning.

Kids who plant a tree plant for posterity.

Proverbs 21:20 (NIV)

In the house of the wise are stores of choice food and oil, but a foolish man devours all he has.

81

Kids who get carried away by their own importance seldom have far to walk back.

Proverbs 11:2

Proud men end in shame, but the meek become wise.

Kids who have burned their mouth now blow on their soup.

Proverbs 14:5,6

A prudent man checks to see where he is going. A wise man is cautious and avoids danger.

Kids who stumble more than once over the same stone deserve to break their shins.

Psalm 40:11,12

O Lord, don't hold back your tender mercies from me! My only hope is in your love and faithfulness. Otherwise I perish.

Kids who sing their own praises may have the right tune but the wrong words.

Proverbs 11:22

A beautiful woman lacking discretion and modesty is like a fine gold ring in a pig's snout.

Kids who tell the truth don't have to remember what they said.

Proverbs 12:5

A good man's mind is filled with honest thoughts; an evil man's mind is crammed with lies.

Kids who are looking for opportunities will find them dressed in work clothes.

Proverbs 12:14

Telling the truth gives a man great satisfaction, and hard work returns many blessings to him.

Kids who don't know where they are going will probably end up some-place else.

Proverbs 28:13 (NIV)

He who conceals his sin does not prosper, but whoever confesses and renounces them finds mercy.

Kids who walk in when others walk out are true friends.

Proverbs 18:24

There are "friends" who pretend to be friends, but there is a friend who sticks closer than a brother.

Kids who speak when they are angry will make the best speech they will ever regret.

Proverbs 19:11

A wise man restrains his anger and overlooks insults. This is to his credit.

Kids who work in summer's heat will not hunger in winter's frost.

Proverbs 10:5 (NIV)

He who gathers crops in summer is a wise son, but he who sleeps during harvest is a disgraceful son.

Kids who dig up facts are getting better exercise than kids who jump to conclusions.

Proverbs 18:13 (NIV)

He who answers before listening–that is his folly and his shame.

Kids who are not afraid to go out on a limb will enjoy the fruit.

Proverbs 1:33

All who listen to me shall live in peace and safety, unafraid.

Kids who weave through traffic may end up in stitches.

Proverbs 16:17 (NIV)

The highway of the upright avoids evil; he who guards his way guards his soul.

Kids who eat forbidden fruit will end up in a jam.

SUCKER BAD BERRY JAM

Proverbs 12:21

No real harm befalls the good, but there is constant trouble for the wicked.

Kids who don't succeed at first should look in the wastebasket for directions.

Proverbs 3:6

In everything you do, put God first, and he will direct you and crown your efforts with success.

Kids who say they are too big to stand criticism are too small to be praised.

Proverbs 23:12

The Lord preserves the upright but ruins the plans of the wicked.

Kids who intend to cross the bridge should have the exact toll ready.

Proverbs 22:3

A prudent man foresees the difficulties ahead and prepares for them.

Kids who expect nothing shall never be disappointed.

Proverbs 13:12 (NIV)

Hope deferred makes the heart sick, but a longing fulfilled is a tree of life.

Kids who cannot stand the heat should stay out of the kitchen.

Proverbs 15:31,32

If you profit from constructive criticism you will be elected to the wise men's hall of fame. But to reject criticism is to harm yourself and your own best interests.

Kids who tune up in the morning stay in harmony all day.

Psalm 5:3

Each morning I will look to you in heaven and lay my requests before you, praying earnestly.

101

Kids who claim to be self-made have relieved God of an embarrassing responsibility.

Proverbs 29:23 (NIV)

A man's pride brings him low, but a man of lowly spirit gains honor.

Kids who stretch the truth usually discover that it snaps back.

Proverbs 26:18,19

A man who is caught lying to his neighbor and says, "I was just fooling," is like a madman throwing around firebrands, arrows and death!

Kids sometimes refuse to let studying interfere with their education.

Proverbs 15:14 (NKJV)

The heart of him who has understanding seeks knowledge.

Kids who are atheists say they enjoy nature but do not know whom to thank.

Psalm 14:1

That man is a fool who says to himself, "There is no God!"

The best mirror is a friend's eyes.

Proverbs 17:17

A true friend is loyal, and a brother is born to help in time of need.

It is better for things to go in one ear and out the other, than to go in one ear, get all mixed up, and then slip out the mouth.

Proverbs 16:23

From a wise man comes careful and persuasive speech.

Kids who raise their eyebrows instead of the roof show self-control.

Proverbs 14:29

A wise man controls his temper. He knows that anger causes mistakes.

Kids who want to strive must rise at five; kids who have thriven may sleep 'til seven.

Proverbs 27:18

A workman may eat from the orchard he tends.

Promises won't butter your bread.

Ecclesiastes 5:4

When you talk to God and vow to him that you will do something, don't delay in doing it, for God has no pleasure in fools. Keep your promise to him.

Kids who would stay "as fit as a fiddle" seldom regret of eating too little.

Proverbs 23:19-21 (NIV)

Listen, my son, and be wise, and keep your heart on the right path. Do not join those who drink too much wine or gorge themselves on meat, for drunkards and gluttons become poor, and drowsiness clothes them in rags.

Kids who laugh at their mistakes will always have plenty of entertainment.

Ecclesiastes 3:1,3

There is a right time for everything...
a time to laugh.

Kids who stay up with the owls all night can't keep up with the eagles all day.

Proverbs 19:15

A lazy man sleeps soundly–and goes hungry!

113

Kids who put their foot in their mouth at least are not stepping on anyone's toes.

Proverbs 10:19 (NIV)

When words are many, sin is not absent, but he who holds his tongue is wise.

Kids who tell you never to let the little things bother you have never tried sleeping in a room with a mosquito.

Psalm 34:6

This poor man cried to the Lord–and the Lord heard him and saved him out of his troubles.

Kids who have a thousand friends have not a friend to spare --Emerson

Proverbs 27:10

Never abandon a friend–either yours or your father's. Then you won't need to go to a distant relative for help in your time of need.

Kids who claim to be self-made show poor architectural skills.

Proverbs 8:13

If anyone respects and fears God, he will hate evil. For wisdom hates pride, arrogance, corruption and deceit of every kind.

117

Kids who hesitate are not only lost but miles from the next exit.

1 Kings 18:21 (RSVB)

Elijah came near to all the people, and said, "How long will you go limping with two different opinions?"

Kids who toot their horn the loudest are in the biggest fog.

Proverbs 26:12 (NIV)

Do you see a man wise in his own eyes? There is more hope for a fool than for him.

Kids who carry a tale make a monkey of themselves.

Proverbs 11:13

A gossip goes around spreading rumors, while a trustworthy man tries to quiet them.

Kids who laugh, last.

Proverbs 15:13

A happy face means a glad heart; a
sad face means a breaking heart.

Kids who faithfully attend church every week will avoid the Easter rush.

Psalm 92:2

Every morning tell [God], "Thank you for your kindness," and every evening rejoice in all his faithfulness.

Kids who lose their heads are usually the last ones to miss it.

Proverbs 16:32 (RSVB)

He who is slow to anger is better than the mighty, and he who rules his spirit than he who takes a city.

123

Kids who don't know whether they are coming or going are usually in the biggest hurry to get there.

Proverbs 21:5 (NASB)

The plans of the diligent lead surely to advantage, but everyone who is hasty comes surely to poverty.

Kids who talk constantly about their inferiors don't have any.

Proverbs 11:2

Proud men end in shame, but the meek become wise.

Kids who kill time should try to work it to death.

Psalm 90:12

Teach us to number our days and recognize how few they are; help us to spend them as we should.

Kids who rise to the occasion should know when to sit down.

Proverbs 12:8

Everyone admires a man with good sense, but a man with a warped mind is despised.

Kids who are quick to blow a fuse spend a lot of time in the dark.

Proverbs 30:33

As the churning of cream yields butter, and a blow to the nose causes bleeding, so anger causes quarrels.

Kids who do things that count don't usually stop to count them.

Proverbs 27:2

Don't praise yourself; let others do it!

Kids who give you free advice are probably charging you too much for it.

Proverbs 14:7

If you are looking for advice, stay away from fools.

Kids who travel the straight and narrow path will find no detour signs.

Proverbs 4:25-27

Look straight ahead; don't even turn your head to look. Watch your step. Stick to the path and be safe. Don't sidetrack; pull back your foot from danger.

Kids who hold a conversation and won't let go are a bore.

Proverbs 25:17

Don't visit your neighbor too often, or you will outwear your welcome!

Reputation is

what you need to get a job; character is what you need to keep it.

Ecclesiastes 7:1

A good reputation is more valuable than the most expensive perfume.

Kids who look for trouble don't need a search warrant.

Psalm 138:7

Though I am surrounded by troubles, you will bring me safely through them.

Kids who go on a diet know that the hardest meal to skip is the next one.

Proverbs 23:20,21 (NIV)

Do not be with...gluttonous eaters of meat; for...the glutton will come to poverty.

Kids who talk too fast often say something they haven't thought of yet.

Proverbs 10:20

The tongue of the righteous is choice silver, but the heart of the wicked is of little value.

Kids who show courage keep their chins up and their knees down.

Psalm 27:14

Wait for the Lord, and he will come and save you! Be brave, stouthearted, and courageous. Yes, wait and he will help you.

137

Kids who have an ax to grind often fly off the handle.

Proverbs 29:20

There is more hope for a fool than for a man of quick temper.

Kids who are boozers are loozers (losers).

Proverbs 20:1

Wine gives false courage; hard liquor leads to brawls; what fools men are to let it master them, making them reel drunkenly down the street!

Kids should give a lot of thought before making a snap decision.

Proverbs 23:23

Get the facts at any price, and hold on tightly to all the good sense you can get.

Kids would rather be ruined by meaningless praise than saved by constructive criticism.

Proverbs 15:32 (NIV)

He who ignores discipline despises himself, but whoever heeds correction gains understanding.

Kids who want to stop a red-hot argument should lay a few cold facts on it.

Proverbs 1:22

"You simpletons!" she cries. "How long will you go on being fools? How long will you scoff at wisdom and fight the facts?"

Kids who blow their own horns are usually off-key.

Proverbs 3:7

Don't be conceited, sure of your own wisdom. Instead, trust and reverence the Lord.

Kids who really want to do something find a way, other kids find an excuse.

TREASURE

DAILY DRUDGE

WEATHER BAD

Proverbs 26:14,15 (NIV)

As a door turns on its hinges, so a sluggard turns on his bed. The sluggard buries his hand in the dish; he is too lazy to bring it back to his mouth.

Real friends are

those who don't feel like you have done a permanent job when you have made a fool of yourself.

Proverbs 21:17 (NIV)

As iron sharpens iron, so one man sharpens another.

Kids who lose their temper should not look for it.

Proverbs 14:29 (NIV)

A patient man has great understanding, but a quick-tempered man displays folly.

Kids who plan their program for tomorrow take the confusion out of the day.

Proverbs 19:2 (NIV)

It is not good to have zeal without knowledge, nor to be hasty and miss the way.

Regardless of policy, honesty is easier on the nerves.

Proverbs 12:13

Lies will get any man into trouble, but honesty is its own defense.

The man with two boys on different Little League teams is a diplomat.

Proverbs 28:26

A man is a fool to trust himself! But those who use God's wisdom are safe.

Kids who know all the answers most likely misunderstood the questions.

JUST ASK ME

Matthew 7:7

Ask, and you will be given what you ask for. Seek, and you will find. Knock, and the door will be opened.

Kids who have a sharp tongue usually cut their own throat.

Proverbs 12:18

Some people like to make cutting remarks, but the words of the wise soothe and heal.

Kids who stand at the head of the line must know where they are going.

Proverbs 11:14

Without wise leadership, a nation is in trouble; but with good counselors there is safety.

Kids who kill time bury opportunities.

Proverbs 10:4

Lazy men are soon poor; hard workers get rich.

The future belongs to kids who prepare for it.

Proverbs 21:20

The wise man saves for the future, but the foolish man spends whatever he gets.

Other Good Harvest House Reading

PROVERBS FOR PEOPLE
by *Vern McLellan*

Proverbs—"electrifying flashes of perception" and "the wit of one and the wisdom of many"—jam this potpourri of provocative points. This hilariously illustrated book is for students, writers, speakers, teachers, business people, and more—anyone who enjoys an instant smile or a clever thought.

PROVERBS, PROMISES, AND PRINCIPLES
by *Vern McLellan*

Here's a colorful collection of thought-provoking sayings, maxims, and quips to give your life and conversation a lift. You'll smile as you read hundreds of topics handled in a readable style that will inspire, challenge, and motivate you as you face the opportunities of daily life.

READ MY QUIPS
by *Vern McLellan*

This is one of Vern's best! Will Rogers once said, "There's no trick to being a humorist when you've got the whole government working for you." Get ready for laughs as our public servants poke lighthearted fun at politics and the American way. You'll enjoy these stimulating one-liners—then double your fun and share them with friends!

WISE WORDS FROM A WISE GUY
by *Vern McLellan*

For day-brighteners, *Wise Words from a Wise Guy* takes the prize. Filled with zany wisecracks, conversation-starters, cool comebacks, and clever illustrations, this book makes a perfect gift for friends who enjoy adding zip and zest to life.

For information on how to purchase any of Vern McLellan's books, contact your local Christian bookstore or send a self-addressed, stamped envelope to:

Mission Services
P.O. Box 472021
Charlotte, NC 28247-2021